A FoxTrot
Kids Edition

by Bill Amend

SCHOLASTIC INC.

ISBN 978-0-545-53738-4

AAAA! copyright © 2012 by Bill Amend.
All rights reserved. Published by Scholastic Inc.,
557 Broadway, New York, NY 10012,
by arrangement with Andrews McMeel Publishing, LLC,
an Andrews McMeel Universal company.
SCHOLASTIC and associated logos are trademarks
and/or registered trademarks of Scholastic Inc.

12 11 10 9 8 7 6 5 4 3 2 1   13 14 15 16 17 18/0

Printed in the U.S.A.   23

First Scholastic printing, January 2013

HA!

HUH?

I GUESS THERE'S ONE PERK TO MOM'S KEEPING THE THERMOSTAT SO LOW.

OH, SHOOT. MY HOT CHOCOLATE FROZE AGAIN.

BOINK!

BOINK!

PLOP!

I DID IT! I DID IT! I FINALLY CAUGHT A POPCORN KERNEL IN MY MOUTH!

AMEND

CONGRATULATIONS. HERE'S THE VACUUM.

OH, FINE. SQUASH MY MOMENT.

DIRT SUCKER 2000

QUINCY SNUCK OUT OF HIS CAGE LAST NIGHT AND CHEWED UP AND ATE MY ENTIRE MATH TEXTBOOK.

THEN THIS MORNING HE PUKED IT UP INTO MY HAIR WHILE I WAS SLEEPING.

JASON, WHY ARE YOU TELLING ME THIS AT BREAKFAST?! DO YOU WANT **ME** TO THROW UP, TOO?!

FORTUNATELY, I HAD MY ENTIRE MATH TEXTBOOK MEMORIZED.

I'LL TAKE THAT AS A "YES."

AMEND

14

HEE HEE HEE...

WHAT'S SO FUNNY?

WE WERE DISSECTING EARTHWORMS IN BIOLOGY CLASS TODAY, SO I TOOK A BUNCH OF THE INNARDS HOME WITH ME IN A PLASTIC BAGGIE.

WHAT FOR?

AMEND

SO I COULD PUT THEM IN JASON'S MITTENS AND GIVE THE LITTLE DWEEB A HEART ATTACK.

WHOA! COOL! WORM GUTS!

OF COURSE, I ALWAYS FORGET THAT HE'S **NOT** A LITTLE DWEEB.

SUPER-GARGANTUAN-MEGA ONE, AT LEAST.

IF I'M THAT BAD ON THE RUBBER MATS, GOING ON THE ICE SHOULD PROVE INTERESTING.

JASON, GET OUT HERE — I NEED TO PRACTICE MY CHECKING.

CLASS, LAST YEAR I NOTICED A PROBLEM WITH THE WAY VALENTINE'S DAY CARDS WERE BEING EXCHANGED.

IT SEEMED SOME OF YOU WERE GETTING LOTS OF CARDS WHILE OTHERS WERE GETTING VERY FEW. I'VE DECIDED THAT AS FIFTH-GRADERS, YOU'RE TOO YOUNG TO HAVE TO DEAL WITH THAT SORT OF STRESS.

SO THIS YEAR, I WANT YOU TO BRING ENOUGH CARDS FOR **ALL** OF YOUR CLASSMATES. THAT'LL MAKE THINGS FAIR.

OF COURSE, THIS MAY INTRODUCE ANOTHER SORT OF STRESS...

WE HAVE TO GIVE CARDS TO GIRLS ?!?

WE HAVE TO GIVE CARDS TO BOYS ?!?

AMEND

I'M SO PSYCHED WE HAVE TO GIVE VALENTINE'S CARDS TO EVERYONE IN THE CLASS.

NOT ME.

THINK ABOUT IT, JASON — IF WE JUST GAVE THEM TO THE PEOPLE WE **LIKED**, IT'D BE AWFULLY EMBARASSING.

HOW SO?

YOU KNOW, YOU AND I SINGLING EACH OTHER OUT IN SUCH AN OBVIOUS WAY.

AH, THE THINGS I'LL SAY TO SNAG A CHOCOLATE PUDDING CUP.

JASON, STOP! THAT'S A FIRE EXIT!

AMEND

JASON, I DON'T THINK YOU UNDERSTAND HOW FIFTH-GRADE ROMANCE WORKS.

WHAT DO YOU MEAN?

IF YOU MAKE YOUR VALENTINE'S CARD FOR THIS GIRL TOO OBNOXIOUS, SHE'S GOING TO THINK YOU LIKE HER. IF YOU MAKE IT TOO NICE, SHE'S GOING TO THINK YOU LIKE HER. AND IF YOU MAKE IT TOO PLAIN VANILLA, SHE'S GOING TO THINK YOU'RE JUST PLAYING HARD TO GET.

WELL, WHAT CAN I WRITE SO SHE **WON'T** THINK I LIKE HER?!

ACTUALLY, I MOVED ON TO SIXTH GRADE WITH FIFTH STILL A MYSTERY.

I SUPPOSE I COULD DO IT IN CODE... THAT MIGHT BUY ME SOME TIME.

OH, MAN, MARCUS, I CAN'T TELL YOU HOW RELIEVED I AM.

I WAS EXPECTING EILEEN JACOBSON TO GIVE ME SOME TOTALLY GOOEY VALENTINE'S CARD, AND INSTEAD SHE JUST SIGNED HER NAME WITHOUT EVEN A NOTE.

HOW WEIRD.

I KNOW. I WOULD'VE BET MONEY SHE'D WRITE ME SOME GUSHY ESSAY.

ESPECIALLY SINCE SHE WROTE ONE TO ME...

SHE SAID ALL THIS MUSHY STUFF IN **YOUR** CARD?!?

AND DARRELL'S AND GREG'S, TOO, I THINK.

...AND MINE.
...AND MINE.
...AND MINE.

I SWEAR, IF VALENTINE'S DAY NEVER COMES AGAIN, IT'LL BE TOO SOON FOR ME.

AMEND

ALL THIS EMPHASIS ON LOVEY-DOVEY NONSENSE... EXCHANGING CARDS... FINDING OUT WHO LIKES WHOM... THIS VALENTINE GUY MUST'VE BEEN SOME SORT OF SADIST!

IT'S LIKE THE WHOLE POINT OF THIS DAY IS TO MAKE GUYS' LIVES MISERABLE.

AHEM.

OK, I'LL ADMIT SOME WOMEN HAVE IT PRETTY ROUGH, TOO.

AND FOR THE LOVE OF MY LIFE, A NEW EXTENSION CORD!

I CAN'T BELIEVE EILEEN JACOBSON DIDN'T WRITE ANYTHING IN YOUR VALENTINE'S CARD.

I MEAN, SHE WROTE MUSHY STUFF TO EVERY BOY IN OUR CLASS.' EMBARASSINGLY MUSHY, EVEN.'

AND ALL THIS TIME WE'D ASSUMED SHE HAD SOME SECRET CRUSH ON **YOU**.

GOOD THING THE FEELINGS WEREN'T MUTUAL, OR THIS MIGHT ACTUALLY BE PAINFUL.

GOOD THING.

OK, SO EILEEN JACOBSON APPARENTLY LIKES EVERY BOY IN THE FIFTH GRADE **EXCEPT** ME...

THAT'S A **GOOD** THING, RIGHT?! I MEAN, I HATED KNOWING EILEEN HAD THE HOTS FOR ME!

...OR, AT LEAST, *THINKING* EILEEN HAD THE HOTS FOR ME.

DON'T YOU MEAN *HOPING* EILEEN HAD THE HOTS FOR YOU?

I WASN'T FUMING OUT LOUD FOR **YOUR** BENEFIT, PAL!

JASON, SWEETIE, WHAT'S WRONG?

I KINDA SORTA TOLD THIS GIRL AT SCHOOL THAT I KINDA SORTA MIGHT POSSIBLY IN SOME INFINITESIMAL, ATOM-SIZED WAY, KINDA SORTA LIKE HER.

I'VE ALWAYS DESPISED GIRLS, MOM! HAVE I LOST MY MIND?! WHAT DOES THIS MEAN?!

WELL, IT PROBABLY MEANS YOU'RE STARTING TO MATURE.

AAAA! NOT **THAT!**

...KINDA SORTA.

OH, MAN — ATOMS ARE SO BIG! WHY DIDN'T I TELL HER "QUARK-SIZED"?!

AMEND

PAIGE, I DON'T THINK YOU UNDERSTAND! I'VE SPENT HUNDREDS OF HOURS TRYING TO DEFEAT THE RED ORB GUARDIAN IN THIS VIDEO GAME!

YOU HAVE TO TELL ME HOW YOU GOT PAST HIM! YOU **HAVE** TO!

DID YOU USE THE FLAMING SWORD? THE SCREAMING SWORD? THE SWORD OF DEATH? THE SWORD OF PAIN? THE AX OF VENGEANCE? THE MACE OF MIGHT? THE RAZOR ARROWS? THE EXPLODING ARROWS? WHAT? WHAT? WHAT?

IF YOU **MUST** KNOW, I SIMPLY WALKED RIGHT BY HIM.

AMEND

WELL, OF COURSE YOU DID ONCE HE WAS DEAD. WAIT! I KNOW! IT WAS THE SWORD OF FURY! AM I RIGHT?!

I DON'T THINK **YOU** UNDERSTAND, JASON...

SO THE SECRET TO GETTING PAST THE RED ORB GUARDIAN IS TO **NOT** ATTACK HIM??

BUT HE'S HUGE! HE'S NASTY! HE'S THE MOST LETHAL VIDEO GAME CREATURE EVER! HE TOWERS ABOVE YOU WITH FISTS LIKE ANVILS! SKULLS LITTER THE GROUND AT HIS FEET!

AND YOU'RE NOT SUPPOSED TO EVEN **TRY** TO TAKE THIS GUY ON IN A FIGHT??

WOW. TALK ABOUT COUNTER- INTUITIVE.

REFRESH MY MEMORY. YOU SPEND **HOW MANY** NANOSECONDS IN THE REAL WORLD EACH DAY?

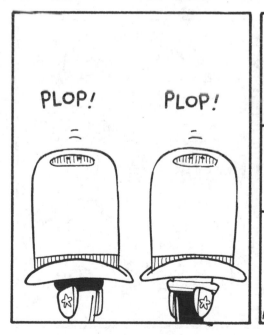

CLASS, GIVEN THAT WE'RE HAVING TORRENTIAL RAINS ALL THIS WEEK...

THAT MANY OF YOU ARE FACING SERIOUS DISRUPTIONS, WHAT WITH ALL THE FLOODING AND ASSOCIATED PROBLEMS...

I FIGURED IT MIGHT BE GOOD TO DO SOMETHING TO TAKE ALL YOUR MINDS OFF THE WEATHER.

POP QUIZ TOMORROW. CHAPTERS 8 THROUGH 53.

AAAA!

AMEND

HI, SWEETIE. HOW WAS YOUR DAY?

LOOK AT ME, MOTHER!

IT'S FREEZING COLD... WE'VE GOT SOME SORT OF ENDLESS RAINSTORM GOING... THE BUS WAS LATE... I'M SOPPING WET... AND I DON'T HAVE TIME TO DRY OFF BECAUSE MY PSYCHO OF A BIOLOGY TEACHER ASSIGNED 46 CHAPTERS OF READING TONIGHT!

AMEND

I COULDN'T *POSSIBLY* BE MORE MISERABLE RIGHT NOW!

GREAT. THE POWER JUST WENT OUT.

OK, GOD, YOU'VE MADE YOUR POINT.

MOM? I THINK THERE'S SEWAGE BACKING UP IN THE BASEMENT...

YOU'D BE PROUD OF ME, DR. TING.

OH?

EVEN THOUGH OUR POWER WENT OUT FROM THE STORM, I SOMEHOW MANAGED TO READ THE ASSIGNED 46 CHAPTERS IN OUR TEXTBOOK USING THE LIGHT FROM BIRTHDAY CANDLES, GLOW-IN-THE-DARK TOYS, AND THE OCCASIONAL FLASHES FROM LIGHTNING. IT WAS A TOTAL NIGHTMARE, BUT I AM **READY** FOR TODAY'S QUIZ!

I MEAN, WE **ARE** HAVING A QUIZ TODAY, AREN'T WE?

WELL, SEE, MY POWER WENT OUT **TOO**, AND SINCE I KEEP QUIZZES ON MY COMPUTER...

AMEND

PAIGE! DON'T! THAT BOOK IS SCHOOL PROPERTY!

BUT YOU'RE RIGHT — I AM PROUD OF YOU.

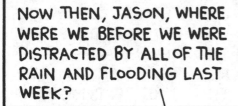

NOW THEN, JASON, WHERE WERE WE BEFORE WE WERE DISTRACTED BY ALL OF THE RAIN AND FLOODING LAST WEEK?

OH, THAT'S RIGHT... YOU HAD JUST LET SLIP THE ADMISSION THAT YOU REALLY DO LIKE ME. SHALL WE PICK UP WHERE WE LEFT OFF?

AMEND

WHAM!
WHAM!
WHAM!
WHAM!

ACTUALLY, I THINK YOU WERE BEATING YOUR HEAD ON THIS LOCKER OVER HERE.

45

TIME TRAVEL?!? ARE YOU INSANE??

IT'S THE PERFECT SOLUTION TO MY PREDICAMENT, PETER.

I FIGURE OUT A WAY TO GO BACK A WEEK, WARN MYSELF ABOUT EILEEN JACOBSON'S LITTLE SCHEME, AND IN DOING SO, PREVENT MYSELF FROM MAKING THE BIGGEST GAFFE OF MY LIFE!

WHAT COULD BE SIMPLER?

WELL, THE TERM "EVERYTHING" LEAPS TO MIND.

LET'S SEE... I GUESS I SHOULD START BY DEBUNKING EINSTEIN...

AMEND

JASON, YOU HAVEN'T TOUCHED YOUR DINNER AT ALL! SORRY, MOM. I'M ON A SUPER CRASH DIET.

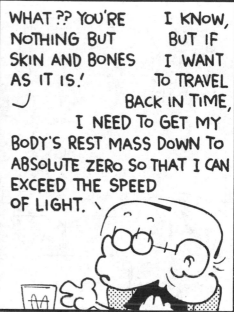

WHAT?? YOU'RE NOTHING BUT SKIN AND BONES AS IT IS!

I KNOW, BUT IF I WANT TO TRAVEL BACK IN TIME, I NEED TO GET MY BODY'S REST MASS DOWN TO ABSOLUTE ZERO SO THAT I CAN EXCEED THE SPEED OF LIGHT.

IT'S A PAIN, BUT THAT STUFF I TOLD EILEEN JACOBSON LAST WEEK HAS GOT TO BE UNDONE.

SO THIS CRASH DIET HAS NOTHING TO DO WITH MY SERVING EGGPLANT LOAF TONIGHT?

TOTALLY A COINCIDENCE. BUT I APPRECIATE THE HELP.

PETER, I'M GOING TO NEED YOUR HELP.

WITH WHAT?

AS YOU KNOW, I'VE BEEN PURSUING TIME TRAVEL AS THE SOLUTION TO MY RECENT EILEEN JACOBSON PROBLEM.

WELL, IF MY THEORIES ON THE SUBJECT ARE CORRECT, I'M GOING TO NEED TO EXCEED THE SPEED OF LIGHT, WHICH IS ROUGHLY 670 MILLION MPH. MOST PHYSICISTS SAY IT'S IMPOSSIBLE, BUT I SAY IT CAN BE DONE.

WHERE DO I COME IN?

I'VE SEEN HOW YOU DRIVE ON THE FREEWAY.

YOU'RE TALKING **NINE**-DIGIT SPEEDS. I'VE ONLY FLIRTED WITH **FOUR**.

WELL, EILEEN, YOU'VE LUCKED OUT.

OH?

I SPENT THIS ENTIRE WEEK RESEARCHING TIME TRAVEL SO THAT I COULD GO BACK AND STOP MYSELF FROM EVER SAYING THAT I LIKED YOU, BUT I'VE CONCLUDED IT CAN'T BE DONE.

AND BELIEVE ME, I WORKED HARDER ON THIS THAN I'VE WORKED ON ANYTHING IN MY LIFE. DAY AND NIGHT, NIGHT AND DAY, SEARCHING, PRAYING, AGONIZING FOR THE SOLUTION THAT WOULD GET ME OUT OF THIS BIND. BUT, ALAS, A HAPPY ENDING WASN'T TO BE.

SO... LOOKS LIKE I'M YOUR BEAU.

AND... I'VE LUCKED OUT **HOW** EXACTLY?

AMEND

FOX, HOLD ON — DON'T TAKE BATTING PRACTICE YET. MY CAR'S IN THE PARKING LOT WHERE YOUR FOUL BALLS TEND TO LAND.

I WANT TO MOVE IT TO SOME-PLACE WHERE YOU WON'T BE LIKELY TO HIT IT.

WHY'S HE DRIVING IT INTO CENTER FIELD?

FOX, AS YOU'LL RECALL, LAST YEAR I MOVED YOU AROUND QUITE A BIT.

I STARTED YOU AT SECOND BASE, THEN MOVED YOU TO LEFT FIELD, THEN CENTER, THEN RIGHT, THEN BACK TO THE INFIELD, THEN BACK TO THE OUTFIELD...

WELL, THIS YEAR, SON, I WANT TO KEEP YOU IN ONE SPOT FOR THE WHOLE SEASON.

SOUNDS GOOD TO ME, COACH. WHERE?

AMEND

NO SPITTING IN DUGOUT!

DON'T FEEL BAD ABOUT BEING STUCK ON THE BENCH.

LOOK AT IT THE WAY I DO— AS AN OPPORTUNITY TO STUDY THE GAME WITHOUT THE ANNOYING DISTRACTION OF HAVING TO PLAY IT.

IF YOU ASK ME, DUGOUT DUTY IS HIGHLY UNDERRATED.

GOLDTHWAIT, GET OUT HERE! YOU'RE BATTING CLEANUP! LET'S GO!

SERIOUSLY. CHEER UP.

I CAN'T BELIEVE DAD CHEERED ME ON LIKE THAT TODAY.

I MEAN, EVEN AFTER HE SAW I WAS JUST A BENCH-WARMER, A FOURTH-STRING-ER, A **NOBODY**, HE KEPT RIGHT ON YELLING, "RAH, RAH, PETER! RAH, RAH, PETER!"

I THOUGHT FOR SURE HE'D THINK I WAS A FAILURE. I THOUGHT FOR SURE HE'D BE DISAPPOINTED.

AMEND

SOMETIMES OUR DAD'S PRETTY COOL.

FOR A GUY WHO SAYS "RAH."

LISTEN, EILEEN, GIVEN MY REPUTATION FOR HATING GIRLS, I WAS HOPING TO KEEP NEWS THAT I LIKE YOU SORT OF OUR LITTLE SECRET.

SAY, ISN'T THAT YOUR PAL MARCUS A MERE 300 YARDS AWAY WITH HIS NOSE BURIED IN SOME BOOK?

HUH?

JUPITER64 TIPS, TRICKS AND HACKS

AAAA! IT **IS** HIM! DON'T LET HIM SEE US TOGETHER! HIDE! HIDE! HIDE!

AMEND

FRANKLY, I SEE EITHER OUR SECRET OR **YOU** BEING VERY SHORT-LIVED.

MAN, THIS SCHOOL HAS WAY TOO MANY PRICKER BUSHES.

HI, MARCUS! HI, JASON! HI, EILEEN.

I SAID HI, JASON.

HELLOOO, JASON... COME IN, JASON... JASON, DO YOU READ ME?... CALLING JASON FOX... JASON?...

WHAT?— I DIDN'T WANT HIM TO SUSPECT THERE WAS SOMETHING GOING ON BETWEEN US!

AND I'M SURE YOUR 10 MINUTES OF STONY SILENCE THREW HIM **WELL** OFF THE TRAIL.

AMEND

PETER, I NEED SOME ADVICE.

ASK AWAY, GRASSHOPPER.

WHEN YOU HAD YOUR FIRST SORT OF MINI, MICRO, TINY RELATIONSHIP WITH A GIRL, WHAT DID YOU DO TO, YOU KNOW, KEEP IT QUIET?

KEEP IT **QUIET?**...

JASON, THE FIRST TIME A GIRL SAID SHE'D GO OUT WITH ME, I ANNOUNCED IT OVER THE P.A. SYSTEM, SENT PHOTOS TO THE SCHOOL PAPER, AND TATTOOED HER NAME ON MY BICEP WITH A RED MAGIC MARKER.

MAYBE I SHOULD WAIT FOR DAD TO COME HOME.

MIND YOU, IT WASN'T UNTIL SEVERAL YEARS LATER THAT A GIRL ACTUALLY **DID** GO OUT WITH ME.

PETER, CALM DOWN. I'LL THINK OF SOMETHING.

CALM DOWN?! SCHOOL IS IN 12 HOURS AND I'VE GOT A BLUE GOATEE ON MY FACE!

YOU'RE TALKING TO A CHEMISTRY WIZ, REMEMBER? I'LL JUST PUT A FEW CHOICE SOLVENTS ONTO THIS RAG AND THAT INDELIBLE INK WILL SMEAR RIGHT OFF!

SUPER STRIPPER

AMEND

ORRR... MAYBE JUST SMEAR.

AAAA! MY WHOLE FACE IS BLUE!

I BORROWED SOME OF MOM'S MAKEUP. I'LL HAVE THAT BLUE INK HIDDEN IN NO TIME.

WAIT A SECOND! I DON'T WANT **YOU** DOING THIS!

THE ONLY MAKEUP JOBS YOU KNOW HOW TO DO ARE MONSTER FACES FOR HALLOWEEN. WHERE'S PAIGE?... SHE KNOWS HOW TO PUT THIS STUFF ON PROPERLY.

NO COMMENTS. JUST DO IT.

NOW, THEN, DRACULA OR FRANKENSTEIN?

HEH HEH... DARE I ASK HOW SCHOOL WENT?

LET'S JUST SAY YOU LUCKED-OUT BIG TIME.

WITH THIS STUPID BLUE INK ALL OVER MY FACE, THE GIRLS DECIDED I LOOKED LIKE LEONARDO DICAPRIO TOWARD THE END OF "TITANIC," WHILE THE GUYS THOUGHT I RESEMBLED SOME ALIEN BEING FROM "STAR TREK."

FORTUNATELY, BETWEEN THE TEASING ON ONE HAND, AND THE GOOGLY-EYED FAWNING ON THE OTHER, IT ALL KIND OF AVERAGED OUT OK.

ODD... I WAS UNDER THE IMPRESSION THAT GIRLS **LIKED** LEONARDO.

IT'S FUNNY. YOU AND I SHARE SO MANY GENES, AND YET...

AMEND

THAT'S H·O·R·S·E.
I WIN.

GEE, WHAT A
FUN GAME,
MR. FIVE·HOOK·
SHOTS·IN·A·ROW.

FAVORITE MOTHER...
WONDERFUL MOTHER...
BEAUTIFUL MOTHER...

FLAWLESS AND WISE—

PAIGE, WITH A BUILD-UP LIKE THAT, I CAN PROMISE YOU IN ADVANCE, MY ANSWER IS "NO."

DO YOU MIND IF I PUT OFF MY HOMEWORK SO I CAN GO TO THE MALL?

I'LL BE HOME IN TIME FOR DINNER.

I'M OBVIOUSLY NOT **THAT** WISE.

FAVORITE MOTHER... WONDERFUL MOTHER...

OUR BROTHER IS SO WEIRD.

OH?

YOU KNOW HOW THE NIGHT BEFORE A MATH TEST, HE SLEEPS WITH HIS MATH BOOK UNDER HIS PILLOW?...

AND HE DOES THE SAME THING FOR TESTS IN ENGLISH, SCIENCE AND HISTORY?...

HE BELIEVES IN OSMOSIS. SO?

WELL, THEY'RE GIVING A BUNCH OF JUNIORS I.Q. TESTS TODAY.

SO THAT'S WHAT HAPPENED TO THE ENCYCLOPEDIA SET.

SCOOT OVER.

SUPPOSEDLY, IF YOU THROW A PLAYING CARD AT THE PROPER ANGLE, IT COMES RIGHT BACK TO YOU.

WOW. FIRST TRY.

MOM, WOULD IT BE OK IF I ATE THE LAST POP TART?

GO RIGHT AHEAD, PETER.

I BOUGHT TWO MORE BOXES AT THE STORE THIS MORNING.

I THINK SHE ASSUMED YOU DIDN'T KNOW THAT.

GO SEE IF WE HAVE ANOTHER GALLON OF MILK.

AMEND

WHAT'S THIS?

PAIGE TOLD ME YOU HAD A ROUGH DAY AT SCHOOL.

SO I FIGURED WHAT BETTER WAY TO CHEER YOU UP THAN TO SERVE YOUR FAVORITE MEAL?

AMEND

I PUT A TOFU PATTY IN A BUN JUST LIKE A HAMBURGER, I CUT EGGPLANT INTO STRIPS JUST LIKE FRENCH FRIES, AND PUT BROWN RICE PASTE IN A GLASS WITH A STRAW, JUST LIKE A CHOCOLATE MILK SHAKE.

OK, SO IT'S **VIRTUALLY** YOUR FAVORITE MEAL.

WELL, YOU'VE SUCCEEDED IN TAKING MY MIND OFF SCHOOL.

CARE FOR SOME BEET-SUP?

AH, THE FAMILIAR SOUNDS OF SPRING.

THE CHIRPING OF BIRDS... THE BUZZING OF BEES...

AND THEN THERE'S MY FAVORITE...

AMEND

THE WHINING OF PETER.

DAD, SERIOUSLY! **EVERYBODY** HAS A GAS MOWER BUT US!

I SWEAR, THIS WARM WEATHER HAD BETTER END BEFORE FINALS.

WHY'S THAT?

IT MAKES STUDYING NEXT TO IMPOSSIBLE, THAT'S WHY!

PAIGE, PART OF GROWING UP IS LEARNING TO OVERCOME THINGS LIKE THE TEMPTATION TO GOOF OFF JUST BECAUSE IT'S NICE OUT.

I'M TALKING ABOUT JASON AND HIS NEED TO THROW WATER BALLOONS.

THIS RED SOGGY PULP IS YOUR BINDER?!

AMEND

UGGH, I'M TOO FULL TO TAKE ANOTHER BITE.

TOO STUFFED TO TAKE ANOTHER BITE.

TOO NEAR EXPLODING TO TAKE ANOTHER BITE.

THEN I GUESS YOU'RE TOO FULL FOR DESSERT.

NO, NO— DESSERTS I SWALLOW WHOLE.

AMEND

NICOLE WAS TELLING ME TODAY HOW HER MOM SERVED LEFTOVERS FOR FOUR DAYS STRAIGHT.

I TOLD HER I COULDN'T UNDERSTAND THAT.

HER MOM WAS PROBABLY BUSY. **YOU** TRY COOKING DINNER EVERY NIGHT.

NO, NO — I COULDN'T UNDERSTAND WHAT A "LEFTOVER" WAS.

I ALWAYS FORGET YOU'VE NEVER KNOWN LIFE WITHOUT PETER.

MOM, ANY CHANCE YOU COULD MAKE AN EXTRA MEAT LOAF TONIGHT?

AMEND

1. Compare and contrast Keats' "Ode to a Nightingale" with Byron's "Don Juan."

4. Compare and contrast Blake's "Songs of Experience" with Wordsworth's "The Prelude."

15. Compare and contrast Shelley's "Ode to the West Wind" with his earlier "Ozymandias."

REMEMBER WHEN YOU READ US THAT ONE POEM THAT SAID THAT "LESS IS MORE"?

I SEE YOU AT LEAST ANSWERED THE QUESTIONS LABELED "YOUR NAME" AND "TODAY'S DATE."

AMEND

JASON, OF **COURSE** IT'S NOT GOING TO BE FULL OF SNOWFLAKES!

LOOK, IT WAS AN EXPERIMENT, OK?

I ALWAYS GET DEPRESSED AROUND FINAL EXAM SEASON.

TELL ME ABOUT IT.

INSANE AMOUNTS OF READING... INSANE AMOUNTS OF WRITING...

INSANE AMOUNTS OF STRESS...

AMEND

I MEANT BECAUSE I VOLUNTARILY TAKE ALL MINE WAY BACK IN SEPTEMBER.

INSANE LITTLE BROTHERS...

THERE'S NOT A
CHANCE OUR LAWN
PETRIFIED OVER
THE WINTER,
IS THERE?

A TANK TOP? SHORTS? TRACK SHOES?

WHAT? ARE YOU TURNING INTO SOME SORT OF BIG RUNNER THIS SUMMER?

IN A MANNER OF SPEAKING.

PETER, I FOUND A COUPLE JOB LEADS THAT I THOUGHT YOU MIGHT—

ODD. I COULD'VE SWORN THAT BOY WAS HERE A SECOND AGO.

HE'S BEYOND ODD, DAD.

TA DA!

AMEND

SPLAT!
SPLAT!
SPLAT!
SPLAT!
SPLAT!
SPLAT!
SPLAT!

CALL IT A HUNCH, BUT I THINK MOST JUGGLERS WORK UP TO THAT MANY EGGS.

I THOUGHT MAYBE I WAS A NATURAL.

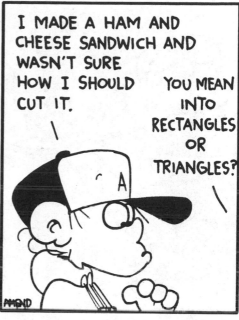

I BELIEVE THE TARZAN YELL IS SUPPOSED TO COME DURING YOUR SWING, NOT AFTER.

WE NEED TO FIND SOFTER TREES.

BACK WHEN I WAS FIVE, I COULDN'T CLIMB A TREE LIKE THIS AT ALL.

WHEN I WAS SEVEN, I COULD MAYBE GET ONTO THAT FIRST BRANCH.

BUT NOW THAT I'M 10, I CAN CLIMB ALL THE WAY TO THE VERY TOP WITH BARELY ANY EFFORT.

I KNEW I WAS TOO OLD TO SEE "TARZAN."

YOUR MOM SAYS IF YOU CAN MOVE YOUR LEG, IT'S PROBABLY NOT BROKEN.

I KEEP FORGETTING TO TAKE MY GUM OUT BEFORE DINNER.

HEY!

I'VE NAMED THIS KITE THE SPF-10,000.

I LIKE HOW YOU WROTE "HA HA" ON THE BOTTOM.

AMEND

PETER, WHAT ARE YOU DOING?

REMEMBER LAST YEAR WHEN I GOT CUT FROM THE SCHOOL FOOTBALL TEAM?

I DANCED A JIG. OF COURSE I REMEMBER.

WELL, I FIGURED OUT WHAT I DID WRONG — I DIDN'T START TRAINING SOON ENOUGH.

WHAT I **SHOULD'VE DONE** IS DO WHAT THE PROS DO, AND THAT'S PRACTICE ALL SUMMER IN 95-DEGREE HEAT.

MIGHT I REMIND YOU THIS SPORT IS POPULATED BY MEN WHO'VE ALL TAKEN BLOWS TO THE HEAD.

RELAX. I HAVE A TRAINER. I'LL BE FINE.

LET'S GO, FLABBY-BOY! 2,000 LAPS! MOVE IT!

DARE I ASK WHAT'S GOING ON OUTSIDE?

PETER'S TRAINING FOR FOOTBALL SEASON.

HE FIGURES IF PROFESSIONAL PLAYERS BENEFIT FROM PRACTICING IN SWELTERING SUMMER HEAT, THEN SO WILL HE. I GUESS HE'S PRETTY SERIOUS... HE'S EVEN PAYING JASON TO COACH HIM.

I HOPE HE'S PAYING HIM A LOT OF MONEY.

WELL, I'M NOT SURE JASON KNOWS ENOUGH ABOUT THE GAME TO BE WORTH TOO MUCH.

AMEND

THAT'S NOT MY POINT.

YOU KNOW, IT OCCURS TO ME THAT IF YOU DIE, I'LL GET YOUR STEREO.

OK, OK, I'LL PAY YOU TWO DOLLARS! JUST COOL IT WITH THESE PUSH-UP DRILLS!

COACH

WHY'S PETER IN A FOOTBALL UNIFORM?

HE'S BEEN HOLDING HIS OWN PERSONAL TRAINING CAMP.

HE GOT THIS IDEA IN HIS HEAD THAT SINCE THE PROS PRACTICE ALL SUMMER DESPITE THE HEAT, IF HE WANTS TO PLAY LIKE THEM, HE SHOULD TOO.

IT'S LIKE 95 DEGREES OUT. THAT'S SOME DEDICATION.

FORTUNATELY, HE GOT A LITTLE SANER AS THE DAY WORE ON.

AMEND

NICE CATCH. NOW LET'S SEE YOU GO DEEP.

MOM? ANY CHANCE YOU COULD TURN THE AIR CONDITIONER UP SOME?

COACH

A

DID THE PHONE RING WHILE I WAS OUT? I'M EXPECTING A CALL FROM HOLLYWOOD.

COOL DUDE

DARE I ASK WHY?

WELL, IN CASE YOU HADN'T NOTICED, THEY'VE COME OUT WITH A SEQUEL TO THAT MOVIE ABOUT A DOG THAT PLAYS BASKET-BALL. HE PLAYS FOOTBALL IN THIS NEW ONE.

SO IT OCCURRED TO ME THAT IF A STUDIO WILL PAY MILLIONS TO FILM AN ATHLETICALLY GIFTED DOG, JUST IMAGINE WHAT THEY'D PAY FOR AN ATHLETI-CALLY GIFTED IGUANA!

COOL DUDE

THAT WOULD REQUIRE YOUR HAVING AN ATHLETICALLY GIFTED IGUANA.

ACTUALLY, I MEANT TO ASK YOU — IS THERE A SPORT THAT INVOLVES A LOT OF EATING AND SLEEPING?

COOL DUDE

145

I HEAR YOUR BROTHER IS TRYING TO TEACH HIS IGUANA TO PLAY SPORTS.

HE THINKS IT'LL GET HIM A MOVIE DEAL.

LIKE THAT BASKETBALL-PLAYING DOG?

EXACTLY. ALTHOUGH HE'S NOT HAVING A WHOLE LOT OF SUCCESS FINDING A SPORT THAT QUINCY'S GOOD AT.

SO FAR HE'S ELIMINATED BASKETBALL, BASEBALL, HOCKEY, FRISBEE, LACROSSE, BOWLING, SKEET SHOOTING AND JUDO.

I'M SURPRISED HE HASN'T ALSO ELIMINATED QUINCY.

THE DAY IS YOUNG.

QUINCY, NO! I SAID THROW THE DART, NOT EAT IT!

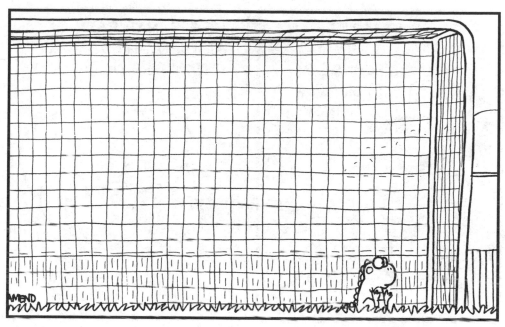

WHO ARE WE TRYING TO KID, QUINCE? IGUANAS JUST AREN'T CUT OUT FOR SPORTS.

LOOKS LIKE THAT BASKET-BALL-PLAYING DOG'S FILM CAREER IS SAFE. I KNOW IT'S TOUGH TO HEAR, BUT SOMETIMES WE JUST HAVE TO BE HONEST WITH OURSELVES.

(SIGH) I THINK IT'S TIME WE GAVE UP THIS SILLY PLAN TO MAKE YOU A HOLLYWOOD STAR.

... AND STARTED WORKING ON A NEW ONE.

WHY'D YOU WANT TO BORROW MY MINIATURE NEW YORK CITY SKYLINE?

PETER, I WANT YOU AND JASON TO GO BUY SCHOOL SUPPLIES TODAY.

I'M GIVING YOU EACH $20 TO SPEND. I TRUST YOU'RE MATURE ENOUGH TO HANDLE THIS MUCH MONEY.

AMEND

ABSOLUTELY. OF COURSE. YOU BET.

FEEL FREE TO CHIME IN.

SORRY. IT'S HARD TO TALK WITH MY MOUTH LIKE THIS.

JASON, DON'T THINK I CAN'T HEAR THOSE CASH REGISTERS GOING OFF IN YOUR HEAD.

PETER, I'M TELLING YOU, ALL WE HAVE TO DO IS RECYCLE OUR NOTEBOOKS AND STUFF FROM LAST YEAR AND WE'LL HAVE $20 EACH TO SPEND ON SOMETHING **GOOD!**

BACK TO SCHOOL SALE

I PROMISED MOM WE'D ONLY BUY SCHOOL SUPPLIES.

PETER, PETER, PETER... DID MY ABSENCE ALL SUMMER UNDO ALL OF MY TEACHINGS?

ALLOW ME TO GIVE YOU A REFRESHER COURSE IN THE FINE ART OF RATIONALIZATION.

YOU KNOW, I BARELY GOT IN TROUBLE ALL SUMMER, EITHER.

TAKE THIS WELL-LETTERED "PLASMA MAN" COMIC BOOK, AN EXCELLENT STUDY GUIDE FOR PENMANSHIP.

PLASMA MAN

PETER, THINK ABOUT WHAT $20 CAN BUY!

ARMLOADS OF COMIC BOOKS! ENTIRE BOXES OF GUM! A 100 PERCENT COTTON "DUKE QUAKEM" T-SHIRT!

AND THAT'S JUST AT THE $20 LEVEL! IF WE **COMBINE** OUR SCHOOL SUPPLY MONEY, WE'LL HAVE A WHOPPING **$40** TO SPEND! CAN YOU IMAGINE WHAT WE CAN GET WITH **THAT**?!

AMEND

I'M HOPING WE CAN AFFORD A BRAIN SCAN FOR YOU.

TWO "DUKE QUAKEM" T-SHIRTS! MY HEART SKIPPED A BEAT JUST SAYING THAT.

JASON, IF YOU WANT TO BLOW THE $20 MOM GAVE YOU ON COMIC BOOKS AND CANDY, THAT'S YOUR BUSINESS. ALL I KNOW IS THAT *I'M* BUYING SCHOOL SUPPLIES.

PETER! NO! PLEASE!

IF YOU COME HOME WITH NOTEBOOKS AND PENCILS AND ALL I HAVE ARE COMICS AND THIS, I'M GOING TO LOOK INCREDIBLY IRRESPONSIBLE! PLEASE DON'T ONLY BUY SCHOOL SUPPLIES! PLEASE? PLEASE? PLEASE?

JASON, I GAVE MOM MY WORD. SORRY.

AND PEOPLE SAY **YOUNGER** BROTHERS ARE ANNOYING.

AND YOU THINK THEY'RE **WRONG??**

HOW CAN YOU SAY NO TO THE SMELL OF BLUE WATERMELON GUM?? DO YOU HAVE A COLD?

HOW WAS SHOPPING FOR SCHOOL SUPPLIES?

WELL, JASON WAS IN TYPICAL FORM.

I IMAGINE HE WANTED TO SPEND THE ENTIRE $20 I GAVE HIM ON COMIC BOOKS AND THE LIKE.

GEE, HOW'D YOU GUESS?

I TAKE IT HE EVENTUALLY CAME AROUND.

ONCE HE SAW THE AISLES OF "PLASMA MAN" NOTEBOOKS AND PENCILS.

IT KILLS ME TO SAY THIS, BUT THANK GOD FOR LICENSING.

PERSONALLY, I WENT WITH THE "BABE-WATCH" LINE OF PRODUCTS.

I FOUND A COUPLE DOLLARS IN MY DRESSER. CAN WE GO BACK FOR MORE?

AMEND

WELL, I'VE GOT MY NEW NOTEBOOKS AND BINDERS LOADED INTO MY BACKPACK.

I'VE GOT MY OUTFIT FOR TOMORROW ALL PICKED OUT AND READY TO WEAR... AND I'VE GOT PLENTY OF PENCILS AND PENS AND BREATH MINTS IN MY PURSE.

AMEND

IT FRIGHTENS ME TO SAY THIS, BUT I MAY ACTUALLY BE READY FOR SCHOOL TO START.

DID YOU FINISH YOUR SUMMER READING LIST?

I ALWAYS FORGET THE LITTLE THINGS.

I THINK YOU DROPPED THIS "WAR AND PEACE" BACK THERE.

YOUR TEACHER CALLED TODAY, JASON.

OH?

SHE SAYS YOU'VE BEEN HIDING MAGAZINES IN YOUR TEXTBOOKS AND READING THEM DURING CLASS HOURS.

SHE SAYS SHE DOESN'T KNOW WHAT TO DO WITH YOU.

ONE IDEA WAS TO LET YOU GUEST-LECTURE.

THE AMERICAN JOURNAL OF PHYSICS ISN'T REALLY A "MAGAZINE," BY THE WAY.

AMEND

THE THING I DON'T LIKE ABOUT USING THE INTERNET IS THERE'S NOT ENOUGH PRIVACY.

I KEEP HEARING PEOPLE TALK ABOUT THAT.

I'M NO COMPUTER WHIZ, BUT AREN'T THERE THINGS YOU CAN DO, LIKE SETTING THE BROWSER TO REJECT COOKIES AND NEVER GIVING OUT PERSONAL INFORMATION?

ACTUALLY, ALL I REALLY NEED IS A GOOD DEAD-BOLT LOCK.

HUH?

I'M TALKING ABOUT PRIVACY ON THIS END, MOTHER.

PETER, MOVE YOUR HEAD. I CAN'T SEE WHAT YOUR E-MAIL SAYS.

AMEND

LET'S SEE...HOW 'BOUT AN ESPRESSO?

NOW THAT I THINK ABOUT IT, I'VE GOT A LOT OF READING TO DO. BETTER MAKE THAT A DOUBLE.

ACTUALLY, COULD YOU MAKE IT A TRIPLE? OR A QUADRUPLE?

HOW MUCH READING DO YOU *HAVE*?

NO, I'M PRETTY SURE "THIRTY-TWO-PLE" ISN'T A REAL WORD.

SO... SHALL WE START WITH CHAPTER ONE AND WORK FORWARD, OR 93 AND WORK BACK?

MISS CHRISTOPHER? WOULD IT BE OK IF I GOT A DIFFERENT COPY OF THIS BOOK YOU HANDED OUT?

WHAT'S WRONG WITH THAT ONE?

IT'S THE COPY MY BROTHER PETER HAD WHEN HE TOOK THIS CLASS.

...AND YOU DON'T NEED ANY EXTRA REMINDERS THAT YOU'RE FOLLOWING IN HIS FOOTSTEPS?

NO, NO — I JUST DON'T WANT HIS LEFTOVER POTATO CHIP GREASE.

GOOD LORD — IT'S TRANSLUCENT.

MOM, WOULD IT BE OK WITH YOU IF I BROUGHT QUINCY TO SCHOOL TODAY?

DEPENDS, I GUESS. WHAT FOR?

WELL, YESTERDAY OUR CLASS WATCHED A FILM ABOUT REPTILES, AND THESE THREE GIRLS KEPT SCREAMING AND COVERING THEIR EYES EVERY TIME A SNAKE OR A LIZARD WAS ON-SCREEN.

AW, SO YOU WANT THEM TO MEET YOUR IGUANA AND MAYBE BREAK DOWN A FEW MISCONCEPTIONS?

AMEND

NO, NO— I JUST WANT TO **REALLY** SCARE THE PANTS OFF THEM.

JASON, DON'T YOU GET ENOUGH OF THAT AT HOME?

AAAA! WHT'S IT LOOKING AT ME LIKE THAT?!

I MEANT, DIAGRAM A WATER MOLECULE ON THE **CHALKBOARD**, JASON.

I SWEAR. SCHOOL COULD BE **SO** MUCH MORE FUN...

HEE HEE HEE.

WHAT'S SO FUNNY?

DAD WOULDN'T GIVE ME $20 TO GO OUT WITH THE GUYS FOR PIZZA, SO I ASKED HIM FOR $20 FOR A HAIRCUT, INSTEAD.

THEN I CUT MY OWN HAIR AND NOW I'VE GOT PIZZA MONEY.

WITH DAD NONE THE WISER.

SPEAKING OF WISDOM...

WITH A COOL AIR OF CONFIDENCE, PAIGE FOX STROLLS ACROSS THE SCHOOL YARD.

HER SIX-PAGE ENGLISH ESSAY IS A WORK OF INSPIRED GENIUS. THE ONLY QUESTION IS WILL SHE GET AN "A" OR AN "A+." SHE DANCES FOR JOY AT THE THOUGHT.

FWIP.!

WITH A WANING AIR OF CONFIDENCE, PAIGE FOX SPRINTS ACROSS THE SCHOOL YARD.

THERE'S NO WAY I CAN GO INTO CLASS AND CLAIM THE WIND STOLE MY ESSAY.

... I'D BE SOME SORT OF LAUGHING STOCK!

OH, MAN — WHERE'D YOU GET THAT?!

GET WHAT?

THAT FAKE ZIT ON YOUR CHIN! IT'S SO BIG... SO WHITE... SO PERFECTLY DISGUSTING...

I'VE BEEN TO EVERY HALLOWEEN STORE IN TOWN LOOKING FOR SOMETHING LIKE THAT FOR MY DECAYING CORPSE COSTUME!

AMEND

OR IS THAT A REAL ZIT?

ABOUT YOUR DESIRE TO BE A CORPSE...

THE, UM, IDEA WAS FOR YOU TO DO THE LAUNDRY ON HALLO-WEEN.

GRAY HAIR NUMBER 18... GRAY HAIR NUMBER 19...

JASON, HONESTLY!

IT'S BAD ENOUGH THAT YOU PLANTED THESE CREEPY SURPRISES THROUGHOUT THE HOUSE THE WEEK **BEFORE** HALLOWEEN...

...BUT THE WEEK **AFTER**?!

ACTUALLY, I PLANTED THEM ALL LAST WEEK. IT'S JUST THAT PEOPLE DIDN'T FIND A LOT OF THEM.

WE FOUND OVER TWO DOZEN! HOW MANY COULD BE LEFT?!

IF I STARTED TO LAUGH MANIACALLY RIGHT NOW, WOULD THAT GET ME INTO TROUBLE?

HOW GOES THE CLEAN-UP OF ALL YOUR LITTLE LEFT-OVER HALLOWEEN SURPRISES?

YOU'LL BE HAPPY TO KNOW THAT I'VE FINISHED WITH THE BASEMENT, GARAGE AND HALF OF THE LIVING ROOM.

AND YOU'RE GETTING EVERYTHING?

YUP. RUBBER HANDS, PLASTIC ZOMBIES, GLOW-IN-THE-DARK SKELETONS, SPRING-LOADED FLYING INTESTINES... ALL OF IT.

AND WHERE ARE YOU PUTTING IT ALL?

UM, THAT YOU'LL BE LESS HAPPY TO KNOW.

MOTH-ERRR!...

WELL, THIS IS THE LAST OF IT.

YOU'RE SURE? I'M NOT GOING TO FIND ANY MORE OF THESE HALLOWEEN TRICKS OF YOURS HIDDEN SOMEWHERE?

NOPE. I SWEEPED THE HOUSE TWICE. THIS LOAD OF RUBBER GHOULS FROM THE LINEN CLOSET IS THE LAST OF MY ARSENAL.

WHAT ABOUT ANY THINGS YOU MIGHT HAVE PLANTED OUTSIDE THE HOUSE?

NOW THAT YOU MENTION IT, THERE WAS THAT FAKE CORPSE I PUT IN DAD'S CAR.

WHERE? IN THE FRONT SEAT? THE BACK SEAT?

AMEND

SIR, ARE YOU AWARE THAT THERE'S A SHOELACE DANGLING FROM YOUR TRUNK?

NO PROBLEM, OFFICER. LET'S OPEN IT UP AND FIND OUT WHY.

GHASTLY EYEBALLS PAINTED ON THE EGGS...

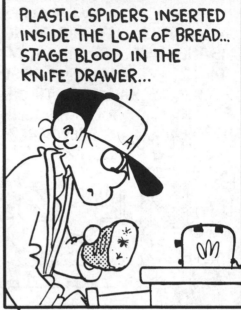

PLASTIC SPIDERS INSERTED INSIDE THE LOAF OF BREAD... STAGE BLOOD IN THE KNIFE DRAWER...

FAKE GREEN MOLD ALL OVER THE BACON STRIPS...

JASON, PROMISE ME NEXT YEAR YOU WON'T GO SO HALLOWEEN GOOFY.

WHAT WAS THAT PART ABOUT MOLD?

CRUNCH CRUNCH CRUNCH

AMEND

Farmer Bob wants to grow dates on 25 percent of his 118-acre farm...

Assuming that train A heads west and train B heads east, on what date will they...

If archaeologist Jones wishes to carbon date one-seventh the number of fossilized dates that archaeologist Smith has dated to date...

I SWEAR, THIS MATH BOOK WAS WRITTEN BY A SADIST.

ANOTHER SATURDAY NIGHT OF HOMEWORK? WOW.

YOU WANTED TO SEE ME?

PETER, THAT WAS MRS. HUMBARGER ON THE PHONE.

SHE SAID SHE SAW YOU DRIVING OUR STATION WAGON DOWN HER STREET TODAY LIKE A RUNAWAY MISSILE.

NO WAY! IMPOSSIBLE! I SWEAR TO YOU, MOM, SHE COULDN'T HAVE!

WE WERE GOING MUCH TOO FAST TO BE SEEN.

YOU KEEP QUIET!

THE KEYS, PETER.

WHAT ARE ALL THOSE CORDS WRAPPED AROUND YOU?

THESE, JASONEZER, ARE THE CABLES OF THE MANY VIDEO GAME CONTROLLERS I SELFISHLY CLUNG TO IN LIFE.

LITTLE BY LITTLE, I BUILT THESE BINDS, AND NOW I MUST LIVE WITH THEM THROUGHOUT ETERNITY.

I HAVE COME HERE TONIGHT TO WARN YOU, JASONEZER.

TO BE MORE GENEROUS WITH MY TOYS?

TO NOT WASTE MONEY ON THIS ONE BRAND OF JOYSTICK. THE FIRE BUTTON IS SLUGGISH.

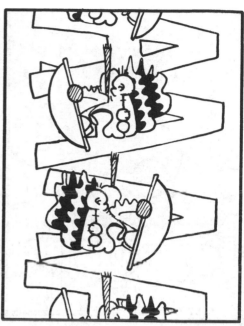

THANKS, MOM AND DAD!
Zeldakong 64
AMEND
THANKS, MOM AND DAD!
THANKS, MOM AND DAD!
A
FOR THE GIFTS, OR FOR GETTING UP AT THIS HOUR?
CAN YOU TELL ME IF I REMEMBERED TO PUT COFFEE IN THIS CUP?